INSIDE ME

My Strong Bones

Lauren
Taylor

QED

QED Publishing

Consultant Jillian Harker and
Mary Lindeen
Editor Alexandra Koken
Designer Melissa Alaverdy

Picture credits
(t=top, b=bottom, l=left, r=right,
c=centre, fc=front cover)

Alamy: 9 Jim Zuckerman, 18
Jupiterimages-Polka Dot
Shutterstock: 4-5 Yuri Arcurs, 6-7
Elena Elisseeva, 8 Joingate, 10 Inara
Prusakova, 11 Olga Lyubkina, 12
Harm Kruyshaar, 13t OKSun, 13b
George P Choma, 14 Yuri Arcurs,
15 Kameel4u, 16b Tankist276,
16t, 17c Cindy Minear, 20 Samuel
Borges, 21t Alex Staroseltsev, 21b
Digital Media Pro, 22 Artbox, 23
Shmel, 24 Grafvision

Words in **bold**
can be found in
the Glossary on
page 24.

Contents

Your skeleton   4

Your bones   6

Breaking bones   8

Healthy bones   10

Joints   12

Your skull   14

Your backbone   16

Your ribs   18

Arms and hands   20

Legs and feet   22

Glossary   24

Your skeleton

Your **skeleton** is strong.

It gives your body its

shape. It holds you up.

It lets you move.

It protects the soft

parts inside your body.

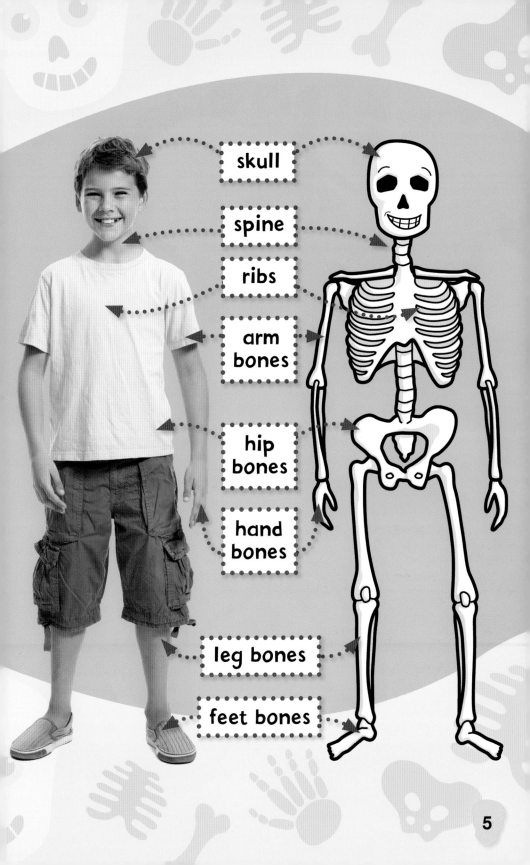

skull

spine

ribs

arm
bones

hip
bones

hand
bones

leg bones

feet bones

Your bones

Your bones are strong.
They are made of layers.
The outside layer is
hard. The middle layer
is like a sponge.

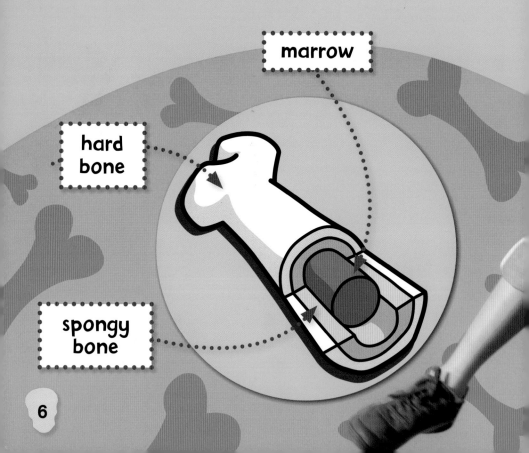

marrow

hard bone

spongy bone

In the centre
of some bones
is a soft jelly.
It is called
marrow.

Breaking bones

Sometimes your bones can break.

If you break your arm bone
the doctor puts a cast on
your arm. This holds the
bones in place as they heal.

Healthy bones

Your bones work best when you are healthy. Move your body. Get lots of sleep.

Eat good food. Milk, eggs and cheese keep your bones strong. So do fish and green vegetables.

Joints

The place where two bones come together is called a **joint**.

A joint works like a **hinge** on a door. It lets bones bend and move.

Your skull

Your skull is made from bones in your head. It protects your brain. It has holes for your eyes. It has a **jaw**.

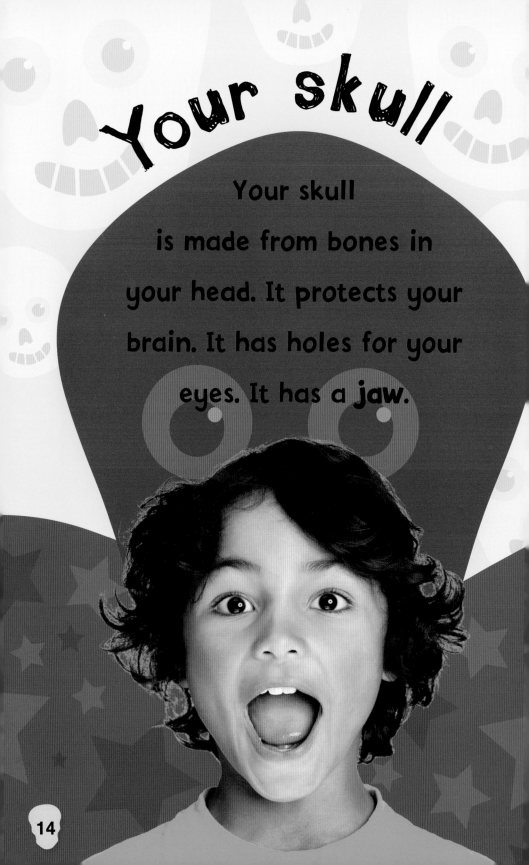

Your jaw lets your
mouth open and close.

Your backbone

Your **backbone** runs down the middle of your back. It is made up of 26 small bones.

backbone

These small bones help you bend. One big bone in your back would make you too stiff.

Your ribs

Your ribs make the shape of a cage. They protect your heart and lungs.

You have 12 pairs of ribs. They are attached to your backbone.

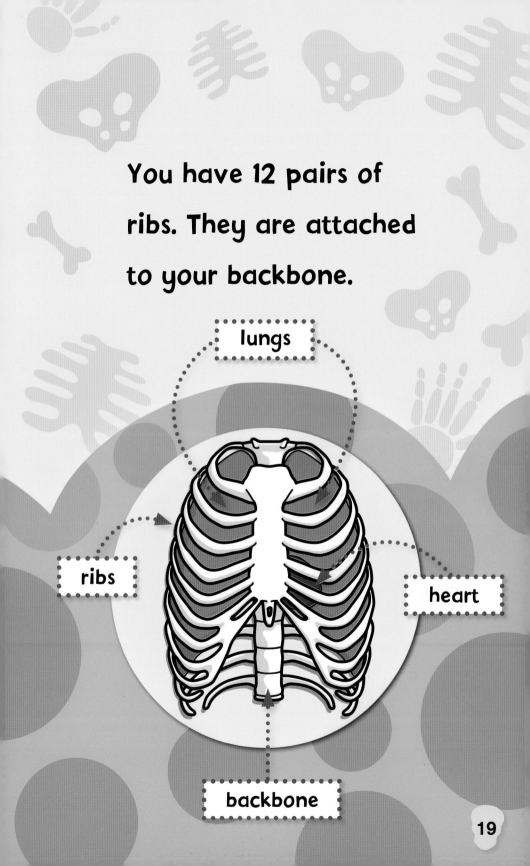

lungs

ribs

heart

backbone

Arms and hands

You use your arms and hands all the time. You pick things up. You write and draw. You throw a ball.

hand

arm

Each arm and hand is
made up of 30 bones.

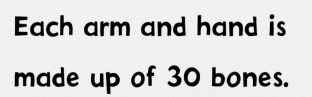

Legs and feet

You use your legs all the time. You walk, run, jump, stand and sit.

The bone in
the top half
of your leg
is the longest
bone you have. It is
really strong!

Glossary

backbone the set of connected bones that runs down the middle of the back; also called the spine

hinge a moveable metal joint on a window or door

jaw either of the two bones between your nose and your chin that hold your teeth

joint a place where two bones meet

marrow the soft jelly inside bones; it is used to make blood cells

skeleton the framework of bones that supports and protects the body of an animal with a backbone